# 30 Minutes
## ... To Negotiate
## a Better Deal

Brian Finch

Kogan Page

YOURS TO HAVE AND TO HOLD
BUT NOT TO COPY

Kogan Page Limited
120 Pentonville Road
London N1 9JN

© Brian Finch 1998

**British Library Cataloguing in Publication Data**

A CIP record for this book is available from the British Library.

ISBN 0 7494 2666 7

Typeset by BookEns Ltd, Royston, Herts.
Printed and bound in Great Britain by Clays Ltd, St Ives plc

# CONTENTS

# PREFACE

We all spend our lives negotiating, to get a better delivery date, a pay rise or a better price and it is surprising how similar are the issues of our personal and business lives. The business deal may have more zeroes on the numbers but the process of negotiating with the plumber is remarkably similar whether you have a leak at home or are installing a new plant in your factory.

This book is intended to provide practical advice for everyone to improve the outcome of all those deals. It is designed for the novice or for experienced negotiators to review what they are doing. The ideas are equally relevant to a charity worker, local government officer, a manager in a large company, an owner/manager – or anyone else. It is possible for all of us to win more and do better deals.

This book describes the preparation that is crucial for success, what happens at the negotiation itself and the aftermath – winning the peace.

**1**

# INTRODUCTION

A few words are needed to introduce five very simple but very important ideas about negotiation:

- what we mean by it
- it is not (necessarily) about being tough
- it is about trading
- it is about achieving mutual benefits
- it is not about defeating an enemy.

The word 'negotiate' comes from the Latin meaning business. It reminds us of the market stall where buying or striking a bargain was an everyday part of living. 'A deal' comes from the equally earthy Anglo-Saxon, meaning a share or a portion. It implies compromise because people often shared part of a booty.

Negotiating and selling are parts of the same process: the difference is one of emphasis, with the salesperson focusing more on meeting the customer's needs, while negotiators emphasize their own needs first.

Successful negotiating is more than toughness. The final result of successful negotiations is agreement: without that there is no deal. But the 'tough guy' approach carries great risk of a breakdown in relationships, hence all those lost deals that should have been agreed.

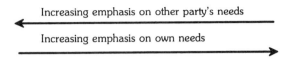

Increasing emphasis on other party's needs

Increasing emphasis on own needs

| SELLING | NEGOTIATING |
|---|---|
| Satisfying customer's needs consistent with own needs | Satisfying own needs consistent with other party's |

## Trading

Negotiation is all about *trading*; something, an exchange must pass each way for it to be a negotiation. If you ask a favour or threaten someone these are not negotiations.

In this trading one party does not have to lose in order for the other to gain. The parties may have different interests that do not conflict or they may have opportunities for mutual benefit. Since the result of a negotiation is agreement and since the parties must see a benefit to agree, negotiation must achieve benefits for everyone.

## Mutual benefits

Discovering, creating and developing 'win:win' situations, where both parties leave the negotiation satisfied, is at the heart of good negotiating. Indeed, the techniques used to achieve mutual benefits are common to all effective negotiating. They include good communication, listening, preparation and planning. Above all, it is an attitude of mind that leads to avoiding negatives. Fixed, unbending attitudes never discover areas of mutual interest. They lose deals that were there to be done.

## Winning

The most irritating thing in negotiating is to agree too quickly; a man, on holiday in Italy, walks around a street market with his wife. They like a beach towel on a stall:

'How much is this towel?'
'25,000 lira.'
'I'll give you 10,000 lira.'
'OK.'

The successful purchaser walks away feeling inadequate and humiliated: he worries that there is something wrong with the towel or that he paid too much. He had not prepared before starting to deal – he had not looked at other stalls.

Of course, it is only in the imaginary world of economists that there is a really open market. Probably no other stallholder had exactly the same towel. In the real world there are further complications; it is hot, you are thirsty and tired, the market is big and you won't search the whole place to save 5000 lira! 'I'll pay an extra 1000 lira to get this done quickly so I can get a drink.'

The question 'who won?' is a meaningless one. If you achieved your objectives then you won and why should you care if the other person won too?

# 2

# PREPARATION

Of all the possible improvements to negotiating the most powerful is devoting a little more time to preparation and to researching, before ever starting to negotiate:

- Any deal is an investment of money, credibility and opportunity. If the outcome is about millions then it is worth investing a great deal of time in preparation. If the deal is about a beach towel, then a stroll to look in other market stalls is still probably justified.
- Every meeting is an investment of your credibility and reputation with colleagues, friends and negotiating partners. It can therefore affect your whole future career.
- Time and energy are scarce resources. While a meeting of two or three people may only take an hour of their time, following up, discussing and recording its outcome may multiply that manyfold.

## Setting objectives

Start at the top. What do you or your organization want to result from these negotiations? These 'wants' are objectives, which then lead to a set of strategies and tactics which you believe will help you to achieve them. Objectives must be:

- *Rational* – Is a desire to win points against the other party – at any cost – rational?
- *Consistent* – Are the defined objectives consistent with your interests and with each other?
- *Achievable* – Setting unachievable objectives for negotiations is fairly common and wastes a great deal of time.
- *Coherent* – Objectives must be sufficiently clear that they can be turned into action plans.
- *Measurable* – If you can't measure your objectives then how will you know when you have achieved them?

What matters to you other than price? What about service, quality and delivery time? Quantify and evaluate each of the other objectives. What level of service is acceptable and what level would you like to receive? Find a way to define it. Maybe it is equipment being in service for 97 per cent of the time throughout the year or never out of service for more than two hours.

However experienced a negotiator you are, it is a good discipline to jot down your objectives.

## Know your opponent or partner

The next key element to preparation is understanding with whom you are negotiating.

### The relationship

What is a 'continuing relationship' worth? Building a relationship with people helps to establish how to speak to each other, to build mutual trust, to understand each other's organizational politics, to find new ways to do mutually beneficial business. However rough the bargaining, the relationship will be preserved if it is to both sides' advantage.

Is this a stand-alone deal or is it a continuing trading

relationship? If there is a future meeting then they may have opportunities to reclaim an unbalanced deal. Bear this in mind when raising the negotiating temperature. As far as a supplier is concerned the 'relationship' often means:

- *Inertia* – Customers continue buying: those long-unchallenged 'relationships' yield the largest profits.
- *Friendship* – It is hard to be horrible to a buddy.

'Relationship' should mean the investment of time and energy in understanding each other's needs so that they can be satisfied with profit to both sides. Never justify anything with the excuse that it 'preserves a relationship'. What exact *interests* may be damaged?

## Assume rational behaviour

Even the utterly mad generally behave in a way that is compatible with their delusions. The negotiator must recognize those underlying values and beliefs and therefore listening and questioning skills are of the utmost importance in such difficult situations.

> You have a dominant position in a negotiation and have humiliated and crushed the other party, who is a weak and pathetic creature. They have no alternative but to submit ... or do they? Suicide is a valid option.

Start with a hypothesis that your negotiating partner is rational and adjust this for possible non-commercial interests and a normal range of emotions.

## Diverse interests

We speak of the 'other party' as if there was one person but there may be several principals, lawyers, accountants and financiers. All these may have different angles and approaches.

11

Try to find out about the *differences* in the other side. Your questioning before and during meetings will help. Notice who says what and think about their motivations. A deal that appears to be going very well can suddenly change direction because someone who said nothing before passes a comment to the chairman outside the meeting. A divided opposition is your problem as well as theirs.

## Understanding

The word 'opponent' is full of confrontation. Before embarking upon the deal it is helpful to understand the other person. What drives them? What are they trying to achieve? What are their sticking points? Form a view of what they want to get out of the meeting and think through what you want.

If you understand what your opponent or partner is trying to achieve then you have the foundations on which to build a negotiating strategy. Consider the customer approaching the market stallholder; it is the end of the day and, having asked at another stall where the next market is, he knows that it is three days off and therefore he has a basis for bidding low.

## Do they want a deal?

People don't always intend to do a deal. They may want information about your business. A competitor may negotiate in order to damage your business through management distraction and encouraging trade rumours. Another may want a deal only if the price is very low. The world is full of people who enter into many discussions in the hope of getting even one bargain over a period of years.

Try to penetrate to the real motivations of the other party:

- give limited information and demand an indicative bid
- demand an introduction from a reputable intermediary

- conduct an auction
- demand a deposit to confirm seriousness.

## Before a meeting

The third element to preparation is to think about the meeting itself.

### Productive meetings

Time is valuable so make each meeting productive. Exchange information beforehand. Don't waste valuable time during it. Anyway, you can't discuss complex documents without having read them before the meeting.

Find out who is to be there and ensure you have the right team to match them. If the other team fields their chairman you may need to do the same.

The place of meeting and its facilities are important. If other people may need to be consulted do you know where they will be? How many people are expected? It does not help your credibility or your self-confidence if twenty minutes are wasted relocating to a bigger room. Do you need telephones, photocopiers, facsimile machines?

What about coffee or food? Refreshment and breaks are essential to maintain concentration and effectiveness. Can you signal when to bring in the sandwiches? It may be in your interests to delay or to bring forward a break.

### Control

Are you clear about what the meeting is intended to achieve? When the meeting turns out to be about something that you are unprepared for, you lose ground. It is not unusual for someone to convene a meeting, ostensibly about one subject, and then to introduce something completely different – perhaps as a 'by the way ...'.

1. Ask beforehand what any meeting is about.
2. Ask for an agenda or submit your own.
3. Refuse to discuss matters for which you are unprepared.

## Positioning

What goes on before any meeting is part of the negotiation. There will be letters, telephone conversations, conversations with third parties. All are aspects of the battle. If the other party has restricted the scope of the meeting or has contacted your business partner then the battle may be lost before the 'armies' ever engage in the meeting itself!

You may find this politicking distasteful. It is probable that throughout the ages generals have found the successful strategies of their opponents underhand and dishonourable.

You may think a first meeting is merely exploratory, with the serious negotiation coming afterwards. This is not so. Each and every meeting sets the starting point for the next: you give and receive information and jockey for position. A point lost may be very difficult to recover.

Preparation includes speaking to colleagues, expert advisers and, possibly, people in the industry. It may not be enough just to pick up a file and scan it briefly before going into a meeting or telephoning someone.

Prepare documents well in advance, not at the last moment. Don't attend negotiations without all the relevant documents because you couldn't find them.

## The bottom line

Know your 'bottom line' before entering into negotiation. This applies equally to buying a beach towel in a market as to an enormous commercial deal. Standing by the market stall clutching a beach towel that has just been acquired is no time to be thinking 'That's an awful lot of money for a towel'.

Clearly, in more complex dealings there are many issues

to be agreed and you don't have to analyse every one in advance: define the key matters that cannot be sacrificed. Being precise about every detail deflects concentration on what is important, and stifles creative thinking. It concentrates the mind on negotiating postures instead.

Concentrate on your interests and not on your postures. Through defining the minimum acceptable results before entering negotiations, you avoid getting carried away in the heat of battle or becoming psychologically committed to doing the deal. While the bottom line is not set in stone and may shift during the course of negotiation, the thrill of the chase or the psychological pressure exerted by the other side may achieve a complete rout unless you can marshall your remaining forces behind those defensive lines.

*Never start negotiating without being prepared to walk away if the deal becomes unattractive.*

---

**Preparation summary**
Who called the meeting?
What is it about?
Who will be there?
What are your objectives?
What are your alternatives?
What is your bottom line?
Do you understand the issues?
   Have you looked at the documents and the numbers?
   Have you spoken to key colleagues?
   Do you need expert advice?
Do you have the necessary authority?
   Have you got or do you need clear instructions?
Who are the other party?
What are their interests likely to be?
Is there a history of past contacts?
   Is there a 'starting point' for this meeting?
What negotiating style fits the circumstances?

---

## It is your meeting

Whoever called the meeting and whether or not you are the leader of your team it is your meeting that you can win or lose. Even a junior member of a negotiating team has responsibility for the success of each meeting and of the deal, otherwise why would they be there? Every member should think about the interests and objectives of themselves and their team and about how to further them. A single sentence uttered at the right time or a novel idea can affect the deal or your career.

## Preparing positions

Imagine that the negotiating parties are two opposing armies. Their fundamental interests are represented by the terrain. Their negotiating positions are represented by the way they draw up their troops. Their objectives are where they would like their troops to be after the struggle. Some of the land they want is occupied by the other party. Their strategy is the grand plan for moving their troops from the current positions to the objectives and their tactics are the detailed feints, attacks and retreats that will achieve the strategy.

Don't get so involved in tactics and trading positions that you forget the big picture. Strategic thinkers win wars.

Negotiators will trade land (interests) until their battle lines have reached a point where they both want to occupy that same bit of land and will have three choices:

1. find a creative way of achieving joint occupation
2. each occupies a bit
3. one side wins

Thinking and preparing beforehand will get you to these final objectives with the minimum of effort.

**3**

# AT THE NEGOTIATING TABLE

## Opening rituals

The rituals at the start of the meeting are important; the introductions establish a 'pecking order'. You may direct your attention to a potential buyer, only to find that his financier, whom you had ignored, comes in with some destructive points. If you had understood the dynamics of their team, which may have been apparent from the introductions, then you might have handled things differently. Listen to who people are, at the opening: not just their names but what they are doing there. If it was not clear, ask.

There will be some social chit-chat before a meeting gets going. This is a part of the meeting and negotiations have started. The parties are establishing some personal rapport, as well as finding out about the other's interests and positions for the negotiation. The two sides are discovering who 'matters' in the other team, whether there are any unrepresented parties, whether the people present have negotiating authority, etc.

The rituals such as discussing connections through family, friends, past experience, etc help to establish identification with each other. With aggressive personalities such matters may have little resonance but, for the most part, they help to oil the wheels of human interaction.

## Speaking first

After the introductions someone must speak and they set the scene for what follows, so those first remarks are important. At a first meeting they may set out the general interests and objectives of the first party. There is often a jockeying for position, with neither side wishing to be too specific too soon.

The natural first speaker is either the 'home team' or whoever has called the meeting and is asserting dominance. If the visitor speaks first then it is an aggressive act; fine if it is intentional. The first speaker also has the opportunity to control the process. 'Thank you for coming along, let me summarize our position for you ... Now, can you set out what you can do to address these problems?' The strength conferred by speaking first is that the respondent must speak to what has been said; to ignore it and say what they had planned to open with is difficult. You may still wrest back control: 'Thank you for that introduction, but before I address the points you have raised ...'

## An agenda

Producing an agenda at a meeting is a powerful way of asserting control and of keeping a meeting 'on-track'. Having written the agenda you have decided what matters will be discussed and in which order. You may be able to leave more contentious matters until later, creating a feeling of success through rapid agreement at the outset. Subjects that you would rather not discuss at all may be left until the end, in the hope that they may be overtaken by time. If you put items at the beginning, on which you are prepared to compromise, this may put pressure on the other party to reciprocate. After some concessions by you, you come to a point that you need to win and you demand they respond with a concession. You may also leave until the end a point that the other party is very keen to discuss, in the hope that they will agree quickly to earlier points in order to get to their item quickly. They may, however, argue that they have made concessions and deserve a response.

Even if it is not appropriate to distribute a formal agenda it is often helpful to write an *aide-mémoire* for your own use.

## Intermediaries and advisers

The intermediary is often present in business deals. Try to deal around them because they add another complicating factor. Intermediaries can sometimes be useful and can achieve things that are beyond the principals:

- The intermediary can act as 'honest broker' if the two principals fall out or get entrenched in their positions.
- Since the intermediary does not have authority to conclude a deal they can explore 'what if?' scenarios without commitment.
- Some intermediaries and advisers have highly developed negotiating skills. If you cannot bring yourself to hold a position and be tough at the negotiating table then use a colleague or an intermediary.

Similar considerations apply to advisers who may bring vital expertise but who can unwittingly stand in the way of a deal. The adviser's own self-interest is to demonstrate usefulness, leading to continuing business. They may not stay silent, even if their services are not presently required. If you are an adviser it is important to be aware of these conflicts inherent in the role itself.

## Seating plans

Seating is important because it:

1. *reinforces status* – Don't sit at the head of a rectangular table, if someone else present takes precedence. Often the second person in precedence sits next to the first. Not observing these customs can irritate and confuse.
2. has a *psychological effect* – It is rare to sit at a round negotiating table because they take up so much space in a room, yet research has shown these are productive in meetings seeking mutual cooperation. They break down the image of confrontation compared with sitting 'head-to-head' across a table.
   - The teams may be mingled if you are negotiating with a view to mutual problem solving or where a number of parties are present.
   - Sitting in clusters at each end of a long table will give a less confrontational atmosphere to a meeting than sitting facing each other.

Sitting across a rectangular table is intimidating if there is a disparity of numbers, particularly when one person is dealing with several. The opposing team will switch the talking, with some people able to think while someone else speaks so they can maintain a fast pace. The sole person has both the psychological pressure and insufficient thinking time.

However tough and clever, nobody is immune to these pressures and being aware of them helps to reduce the effects. Resist making definite commitments under pressure – 'Let me come back to you on that.' Make time to think by asking to check with colleagues; while on the telephone there is time to think and also to exchange ideas.

If you are holding a negotiation in your office but want to

promote a collaborative atmosphere then walk around your desk and greet them as they enter, then sit on their side of it. Don't sit on the desk as this is intimidating behaviour signalling territorial ownership (of the office) and your higher status (sitting higher).

## Finding mutual interests

If you have a closed mind then you will not find mutual benefits. You must be looking for them. If you are negotiating only on price, then there is really no scope for mutual benefit. You want to pay X and they want to get Y. It is a question of bluff and counterbluff. However, even here, there may be possibilities overlooked. In the example of the tourist buying a beach towel at the market there was a chance to get mutual benefit from bulk purchase.

The more issues that come into a negotiation, the greater the possibility of finding mutual benefit. Typical issues are price, quality, service and delivery and each dimension may be more complex than it appears at first sight. Consider service. I demand a 30 per cent price reduction for equipment maintenance. The service company refuses but responds 'Do you need service on Sundays and late at night? How quickly do you need an engineer on-site?' In the end we do a deal based on shorter hours of cover, that meets our needs, yet is cheaper for them to provide. Price has many dimensions. We undertake to pay within 30 days of invoice, whereas previously we stretched to 40 days. Other possible dimensions of price include payment:

■ dependent upon sales or profitability
■ in kind/cash/shares, etc
■ in a tax-efficient manner.

Steps to inventing solutions are:

1. Identify the real objectives of each party.
2. Translate these into things you can deliver.
3. Look for trade-offs.

Mutual benefits are discovered both through preparation and through the meeting process itself. The preparation enables you to start a meeting with a list of things to trade. Look for the less obvious objectives that emerge in a meeting that offer the opening.

Once mutual interests have been created to break an impasse, the question arises of to whom the value belongs. Do not agree too quickly. The mutual part of the benefits has been achieved and you are now firmly in combat territory: their gain is your loss and they are unlikely to have suggested something that splits the new value evenly. Whatever their offer, propose something slightly different, to test them. They may be feeling the same relief at success that you are.

## Do mutual benefits really exist?

Imagine two shipwrecked sailors marooned on a liferaft in the middle of the ocean, without a sign of land or of another ship. The parallel is drawn with negotiators; if the two can cooperate they ensure the survival of both of them.

While this is an interesting story: it might be best for one to throw the other overboard in the night and not to share limited provisions. In negotiation don't get carried away with the idea of mutual benefits and lose sight of the possibility that conflicting interests may outweigh shared ones.

# 4

# COMMUNICATIONS

## Listening

Listening is the beginning of all communication:

'No one means all he says and very few say all they mean, for words are slippery and thought is viscous.'

We speak at about 125 words per minute but can take in information at four or five times this rate. The mind is therefore prone to wander. The good listener uses this 'extra time' to think about what the speaker is saying. What do they really mean? What conclusion are they driving towards? Repeat back what you think you disagree with: 'So, if I understand you correctly you are saying ...'

If you don't listen effectively then you miss crucial information. You will also miss nuances and body language that hint as well as clearly spoken words.

There are two types of 'not listening' that we all suffer from, more or less often:

1. *Switched-off mode* – attention declines after just a few minutes and is affected by factors such as a heavy lunch or a late night. We take in fewer of the words that are spoken and understand less. Perhaps we begin to think

about what we are going to say rather than about what the other person is saying. We interrupt them to respond or put in our own view or change the subject. This is aggressive behaviour. It signals that we don't care what they have to say and this is likely to harden their position.

2. *Listening through a filter* – Our preconceptions and prejudices filter new ideas and information. We hear what we want to hear and edit out the rest. We deal with complex situations by simplifying them so we ignore what is said that does not fit with what we expect. Dealing with our own closed minds or selective listening is hard but the techniques described below can help.

## Active listening

The term 'active listening' describes a process of repeating what someone has said back to them, in your own words, in order to check understanding, to demonstrate that you have been listening and to show some empathy.

1. *Ask questions to test understanding* – 'So, does that mean...?' This checks that you really do understand and also sends a positive message that you are listening and interested. Phrases such as 'Yes, I see' do not help listening. They can come out when you are not listening and don't see.

2. *Summarize what the other person has said in order to check understanding* – Any feedback you can give will make the discussion less tedious for you, helps you to concentrate, allow you to seek mutual benefits and send positive messages to the other person.

3. *When it is your turn to speak always say something that relates to what the other person has said* – This ensures that you listen to and think about what the other person has said. If you completely ignore what they said you

insult them and encourage them to respond aggressively. Even if they are talking nonsense, respond to it.

4. *Make eye contact* – It is harder for attention to slip away if you are looking at someone and they at you. You can also pick up visual clues to their thinking.

5. *Try not to interrupt but don't let the other person speak for too long* – The longer the other party speaks, the more likely your attention is to wander, so ask questions, summarize and respond frequently. If you feel your attention wavering that is the time to say something.

Taking notes is a useful technique. It forces you to think about what to write down but it has two big disadvantages: it makes eye contact more difficult and, when you are writing, you cannot speak.

Don't allow meetings to be interrupted unless unavoidable. There are occasions when you just have to take a call even at the risk of causing offence. But if you must take the interruption, do it outside, keep it short and apologize.

## Talking

The other party may be very sensitive to nuances that you may or may not have intended. It is possible to lose your position completely because of a misunderstanding or offence that you did not mean to give. Choose words carefully and, equally, listen carefully.

The person who talks and does not listen is often outwitted by the clever listener. Don't talk for more than a couple of minutes before getting the other party to respond, because:

■ The other party may become bored and switch off, leaving you amusing yourself. Asking questions forces them to pay attention.

■ It is hard to talk and observe at the same time.

Since the purpose of speaking is to communicate, use language the other person will understand. Avoid jargon: they may not tell you that they haven't a clue what you are talking about. Repeat and summarize what you say, and get the other party to repeat key points that you think you have made.

Key points in talking effectively are clarity and brevity, that have been dealt with earlier, also:

- *Tone*, which refers to the inflections of voice, gesture and posture that convey as much meaning as the words. Is your tone effective? Do you raise your voice without really thinking about it?
- *Colour*, which is the way we link what we say to people's interests and make it comprehensible and personal to them. An example would be using banking examples for bankers and sales examples for salesmen.

'Flags' in speech can help effective communication. 'Now, this point is of the utmost importance to us ...' They won't misunderstand that!

A powerful personality may walk from the meeting having won every exchange – but lost the war. Don't debate, this is not a game, it is not about being right, it is about getting someone to do what you want them to do and logic may not be the right approach.

## Don't talk too much

*When the point is won stop the discussion ... carry on and find you have plucked defeat from the mouth of victory.*

- Even when the deal is done, a foolish word can ruin it.
- Don't continue arguing when the other party is ready to agree – the moment may be lost.

- Don't give the other party an irrelevant issue to exploit. They will concentrate on this and, for no good reason, the battle is lost.
- Don't offer three arguments when one would do and advance the strongest argument first.

## Questioning

Successful negotiators find out a lot about the other party before and during meetings. You will conduct effective questioning in parallel with the dealing but be subtle: this is not an interrogation. Consistently successful negotiators seem, often unconsciously, to broadly follow the approach outlined below.

Start with broad questions, finding out all the background that is relevant *to the other party*. Then specific enquiry and discussion homes in on important issues that provide material for trading.

### Open questions

Start with open questions. These do not suggest an answer and do not allow for a yes or no response. The other person must give some information to you and is drawn into talking and may tell you things that you would not have thought to ask about. It is, therefore, a powerful way to seek leads to follow up with other questions. An example of an open question might be 'Where do we take things from here?' Your question invites a whole range of responses.

### Closed questions

Closed questions, in contrast, are very precise and specific and may call for a yes or no response. Their place in any conversation may be where you need a precise answer, such as 'Are you able to complete by next week?' The answer won't give you clues to mutual benefits but none are being sought at this stage.

## Context

Pose context questions that find out something about the person, the organization, what their plans are, etc. These should be open questions: 'How are you thinking of expanding further beyond the purchase of this company?'

## Interests and problems

From these you follow up along avenues opened by their responses to seek interests and problems. 'So, does that mean that you are looking for distribution overseas as well?' You store the response for later or you may follow up immediately to demonstrate a shared interest or mutual benefit.

## Benefits

The most powerful statements in selling and in negotiating are those that show how you can satisfy the needs of the other party. 'Although we can't meet your original price, you have explained how important future supply is to you and we are uniquely placed to meet your needs there.'

## Summary

The shift from questions which encourage a discursive answer to detailed questions is sometimes referred to as a funnel technique. You narrow the focus of enquiry until you concentrate on a precise need, problem or interest.

As with all such mental 'models' it is also important to appreciate its limitations. During discussion further clues may lead you to other lines of enquiry.

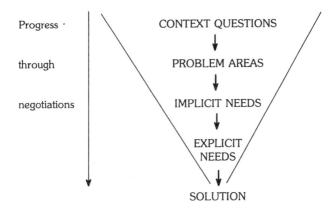

## Keep probing

Throughout negotiations seek clues to the real position of the other party. Never forget questions and switch entirely to bargaining: questioning and testing understanding should continue until the deal is done.

The market or the needs of the parties may change while you talk. Indeed, the whole process of negotiation is about moving positions, so keep tracking how the other party has moved. Prepare to have options ready *before* entering negotiations.

The best negotiators think quickly on their feet and adjust their positions as their understanding of the other party improves. The rest of us use recesses to consider new information or defer an issue until later, to create time to think about new information.

## Groups and teams

A negotiation involves at least two people and often more: lawyers, accountants, colleagues, etc. A group may achieve more than two people can through its 'group mind' which comprises the wisdom and knowledge of all its members. However, it is not one mind and has to communicate between its parts. With more people at the meeting the complexity of relationships grows dramatically; with two people there is only one relationship, with three people it rises to three and with five people it has become ten.

Resist expanding the team to include people who do not have to be there. Teams should ideally be no more than three or four people.

In complex deals where there must be many advisers or where a number of parties may be involved, you need 'rules of engagement' made clear to all. Discuss new ideas and resolve any differences *outside* meetings. Designate spokesmen to speak inside meetings. If these simple rules are not followed then the other party finds it hard to know who to negotiate with or what view they are discussing.

Ensure you set a clear and complete brief and know the essential points and priorities. The chairman may give only a couple of throw-away lines as the extent of the brief; you are then left to carry the responsibility. Get a good brief, know the essential points and priorities. Write your own understanding of the brief and send that to the chairman.

Keep your own team informed of what is going on when they are not present. Remember decision makers who are not present, such as the chairman or the banking consortium. You cannot refer back constantly, which undermines your ability to negotiate, but they must be kept in the picture. The strong negotiator tries to avoid promising successes before they are certain. Go to the chairman for approval of a final deal in the confidence that it will be given assent.

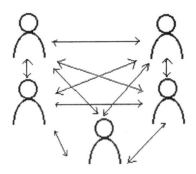

## Misunderstandings

Misunderstanding and different interpretations are rife in negotiation and are the most frequent block to success. The best way to avoid misconception is to address issues directly because people are usually less sensitive than you may think. 'I was a little confused by your replies to some questions about the property, can I just run over them and check that I understand ...?' There are two powerful techniques available for avoiding these communication errors.

### Check understanding

During the discussions check, every now and then, that your understanding is indeed the same because it very frequently isn't.

Fred, the managing director, asked his operations director, John, to reduce stocks quickly in the shops in order to help the company's cash flow. John had heard this sort of thing before. 'Yes, Fred,' he replied, wearily.

Simple – he agreed, didn't he? Well, I was there and I didn't think he did. Surely 'yes' is a straightforward word

31

whose meaning cannot be mistaken? No.'Yes' can mean;

Yes – I hear what you say

Yes – yes, yes, calm down, we'll talk tomorrow when you are more rational

Yes – I'll have a go

Yes – I'll make it happen

In this case it meant 'I will make a show but there is no chance that we can meet that target.'

Often two parties think they have a mutual understanding but reach a critical point in discussions only to find they do not. Since you never know what you don't know, the only solution is to check and recheck understanding of important points. 'So, let me confirm that, we agree that ...'

While it can be irritating if these checks are too frequent, people are also pleased to know that you were really listening. You can check more than you think. There are also lots of variations to be tried: 'I'm sorry, I'm not sure I understood that. Are you saying ...?'

## Summarize

'Let me summarize where I think we have got to ...' You can identify and resolve misunderstandings and by emphasizing what has been agreed you create a momentum of progress. You focus everyone present on the matters still to be resolved and, as the person who summarizes, you influence the direction of discussion.

Write a summary of an important meeting which you should send to everyone who was present. If necessary get them to confirm it as a correct record. List:

1. areas of agreement reached
2. areas still to be resolved
3. what the next step is.

# 5

# BODY LANGUAGE

Many studies claim to show that over 50 per cent of the messages we convey are through gesture, expression and posture. This is in addition to the messages conveyed through tone of voice. Whether it be banging the table with our fists, directing an angry stare or looking puzzled, it is hard to deny the importance of this side of communication. The astute dealer is always alive to body language but don't concentrate so much on it that you don't pay attention to what is actually said.

Look and listen and think about what the other person says, how they say it and what they do. Be aware of yourself as well. If you recognize a pause in the wrong place or a phrasing that implies weakness then immediately look for a way to counter the impression produced. The game is not lost until the encounter is over. Many of these signals do not require a deep study of psychology. They require awareness, some common sense to recognize meaning and a readiness to do something about the signals that are sent and received.

---

One of the most frequent signals in conversation is repetition. It can mean that a point matters a lot to the speaker or that they are lying.

'What I tell you three times is true.' (Lewis Carroll, *The Hunting of the Snark*)

---

Some expressions and gestures are particular to specific cultures, while others are common to the entire human race, such as smiling or the bared teeth of anger. A smile can be faked: it can mask anger and aggression. However, the way we stand and what we do with our hands is harder to control. There is another layer of body signals, of greater subtlety, such as the narrowing of eyes, the shape of the smile and even the contraction of the pupils of the eye, which may also betray the real feelings of the smiling negotiator. Most of those gestures are universal.

If we can interpret this involuntary commentary then our negotiating position will be stronger. We could recognize a lie, whether our arguments were being accepted or whether the other party was unreceptive and adjust our behaviour accordingly.

We all recognize a lot unconsciously, which is how we get a feeling that someone is lying or that they are bored. In lying, people's expressions, postures and gestures convey contrary messages to their words and we intuitively recognize the disparity. To negotiate more effectively, be sensitive to these signals, whether by paying more attention to your feelings or by consciously observing and thinking about the gestures and expressions we see.

Signals don't appear singly but in clusters of several that reinforce each other. Don't rely upon just one gesture that may be misinterpreted but take the wider evidence available. *We frequently say things we don't mean and mean things we don't say. How easy it is to imply things we don't mean!* Interpretation of the 'sub-text' of communication is inaccurate. Don't rely upon what you think is going on under the surface without checking your interpretation.

Typically, someone who is lying will avoid your eye and may look downwards. They may touch their faces around the mouth and have the palms of their hands hidden from you. The other party may adopt a tone of voice of great sincerity and look you steadily in the eye in order to reinforce the deception of their words. If you look away from that gaze you may see signals they are unable to control, which give the game away.

Recognition of body language also help to understand our own feelings. If we feel irritated by someone, could it be because they are leaning back in their chair, with head slightly tilted back (looking down their noses at us), perhaps with hands together making a shape like a church steeple, or with hands behind their head? We may both be standing up and the other person is holding their jacket lapels, waggling their thumbs at us. These are all gestures of superiority and might explain our annoyance. Understanding this, we may be able to handle it better.

During a meeting you may find you don't like someone. Is the other person unpleasant or is there some unconscious signal they are sending that is annoying? They may, for instance, be terse and dismissive of points that matter to you, which can be highly offensive. They may doodle energetically while you are speaking, or sigh as you speak, suggesting perhaps that you are a fool. They may not mean to give offence and it may not be in your interests to take it. Once you recognize what is annoying you can deal with it either by an effort of self-control or by calling attention to it. 'Excuse me, John, you aren't paying attention to these points but they are important to us ...'

There are cultural mannerisms that differ between nationalities and cultures. For example, the appropriate space to leave between yourself and the person you are talking to varies between cultures. In Japan or the USA it is common to stand closer than it is in the UK and much of the rest of Northern Europe. Be sensitive to differences and observe what happens in a strange culture. One of the problems between the Americans and British is the common assumption that, because of a common language, cultural norms are also the same.

Other typical gesture clusters to be aware of in negotiation include:

| | |
|---|---|
| Assessing and evaluating | Head on one side, hand to chin |
| Resistant/blocking out/ defensive | Crossed legs and arms. The figure 4 shape made by crossing the legs is interpreted as being particularly aggressive/defensive |
| Negative | As above, also head inclined down. The head supported heavily by the hand indicates boredom or detachment |
| Positive | Leaning forward, hands palm upwards |
| Restrained emotion | Gripping arms of chair |
| Hostile | Clenched fists |
| Superior/aggressive | Hands on hips, legs wide, direct upright pose 'head to head' |
| Honesty/openness | Palms of hands displayed, meeting eyes, uncrossed legs, leaning forward |

Understanding the probable meanings behind another negotiator's body language is helpful but does not guarantee success. Recognizing that someone is probably feeling negative towards a proposal does not provide a means of overcoming their objections.

## Self-control

We all have personal mannerisms which may not send the signals we really want to convey. I tested the power of body language on meeting an acquaintance in the street. I realized, as we chatted, that my hands were on the back of my hips – pushing my shoulders up and chest out. This is an aggressive sort of stance which emphasizes our size. The other person, who is smaller then I am, had crossed his arms in a defensive gesture. Taking my hands off my hips, he dropped his arms too.

After a particularly hectic and tiring time, my wife and I were having dinner at home quite late at night. My wife spilt something on her new shirt and I, unhelpfully, pointed out that this was an unsurprising occurrence if she leaned back in her chair while eating. I was leaning back in my chair, with my head back and my hands behind my head in the classic 'smart arse' pose. I moved quickly and am delighted to report that, as this book goes to press, we are still married.

Try experiments of this sort too; noticing your own stance, observe what the other person's gestures are – change yours and see what response there is. You quickly become more aware of your unconscious parallel conversation.

Avoid habits that irritate such as doodling or staring into space, out of the window or at the ceiling (what fascinating tiling) or closing your eyes as if concentrating (or taking a nap?). Don't clean your fingernails, drum your fingers or crack your knuckles. How you sit matters too. Don't slide down your chair, keep crossing and uncrossing your legs or throwing a leg over the arm of the chair. Don't fiddle; with pens, jewellery, the coffee cup, tea spoon or sugar cubes. It is pretty irritating to keep examining your tie, picking at lint, cleaning your glasses or adjusting your cuffs.

There may be reasons for showing indifference or disapproval through one of these signals but do you really mean to? Be there in mind and gesture as well as in body. If you want to show attention and interest, sit upright and forward and meet the other person's eyes.

# 6

# STRATEGIES AND TACTICS

An eternal dilemma of negotiating is whether to bid high or bid low.

## Bidding high

Why bid high? A first bid close to your maximum attempts a shut-out of competitors and any further negotiation. 'This is my final offer and we must complete by next Friday.' You have reduced your scope for rebidding and increased the risk of losing the deal. The other party may not believe that it is your maximum and it may raise their expectations. You must make them believe it is your last bid.

In most negotiations the parties need the psychological satisfaction of improving the deal, which is one reason for allowing some room for haggling. You make an offer and it is accepted – you immediately worry that the offer was too high. Therefore even if the first offer is near the maximum available, leave a little room for manoeuvre.

## Bidding low

Always be ambitious in the targets you set yourself. You may guess, but cannot know for certain, what the other party is looking for. Therefore you must set a high target on the basis that *if you don't ask you don't get*. It is often a surprise what can be achieved if you ask for it. People who set more ambitious targets achieve better results.

If you bid too low the other party may conclude that you are not really a serious contender and may turn to one of their other options. Your chance to make your best offer is then lost.

The primary reason for bidding low is therefore to give you the advantage of being dragged uphill towards the maximum price you were prepared to pay. The theory is that this gives a better outcome for you. When bidding low, pitch it at a level that is still defensible. The bid therefore goes hand in hand with a justification and planning how to deliver it.

A low offer may result in signs of distress from the other party: follow up a low bid in order to retain the initiative. However, *don't lose your nerve!* They may dismiss your low offer. Such a response is easy, costs them nothing and you may panic: don't. Your low bid has four stages:

1. *Making the offer*
2. *Explaining* – Explain why the offer is fair and why the deal is good for them. Do not be apologetic.
3. *Testing the response* – Find out what parts of the offer are unacceptable (or acceptable). Ask them to explain how they feel about your offer and probe their response. 'Am I right in thinking that you find our proposed payment terms attractive?' Explain how you got to your offer. Tell them that their asking price does not seem realistic and ask what their objectives really are. If they respond then you are moving again.
4. *Following Up* – The other party genuinely does find your offer ridiculous. Now do you panic? Never panic. The bid

was low: you are prepared to offer more; you must get negotiations moving again, but how?

- *Make an instant concession, dressed as an explanation* – 'If you can move on the very tight delivery requirements and the sixty-day payment terms then we would be able to discuss the price.'
- *Ask for a recess to consult colleagues* – If you don't know how to continue give yourself time to think while keeping in the game.
- *Tough it out and see what happens* – You could be wrong: they may be bluffing.
- *Give in* – If there is no alternative consider retreat as the very last option.

## Bidding first

The first bid sets the running and takes the initiative. The first offer is seldom the final one. If you bid low, bid first. If you offer a shut-out, then bid first. In many cases you will want to have an idea of what the other party wants and will be happy for them to take the initiative. I prefer to get my bid in first to gain and keep the initiative.

The first bid sets the tone for the negotiation. If you are able to establish that the starting point is lower than the likely outcome then you must be dragged uphill towards it and the result should be a lower price than if you started from the other direction.

## Bidding last

The risk of bidding last is that the other party makes an unacceptable suggestion and then feels unable to move from it. They now have to be dragged towards an acceptable deal. It may be an advantage to bid last in complex negotiations to give time to find out more.

# 7

# DEALING

The interchange between the parties is the focus of negotiating that all this preparation leads up to. This is the heat of battle in which brave theories may not work.

## Aggression

In the real world aggression is a common problem to be countered as well as a weapon to employ at times. However, it is dangerous and must be used with care.

### Defence

One party is often not interested in seeking mutual interests. They want to win and they apply a range of techniques to 'put one over on you' no matter how hard you try to search for those mutual advantages. How do you cope?

Is cooperative behaviour worth while for you? There may be no possible mutual benefits, such as when price is all-important. This is particularly true when there will be no continuing relationship. Cheating usually only occurs when the parties know they will never meet again.

### Deflecting aggression

Aggressive techniques that can be used against you include; extreme demands, shouting and banging the table, threats, bluff – take it or leave it, good guy/bad guy routines. This behaviour is meant to get you to make unplanned concessions through creating discomfort and uncertainty. It is also aimed at lowering expectations to make you feel you won't get what you aimed for. The broad types of response that the victim of aggression may offer are:

- *Making unplanned concessions* – The aggressor won.
- *Aggressive response* – This leads into a cycle of aggression until discussions break down.
- *Walk-out* – Both sides may lose what could have been a successful deal.
- *Deflect the attack and move to productive negotiation* – Above all, don't be a victim.

## The cycle of aggression

Many people try to blast the opposition out of the way by a full frontal assault. It may work when a dominant personality confronts a more compliant type or when an powerful negotiating position meets a weak one. The aggressive approach is usually a mistake.

The first consequence is that it encourages a mirror image on the other side. The other party sees the attack as personal and becomes intransigent; it is hard to switch to a problem-solving approach when you are eyeball to eyeball. In the middle of a difficult negotiation with an obdurate and unpleasant person you lose your temper and call the other person a name. You feel better but have you advanced towards your goal or have you damaged your interests?

## Escalation

The negotiation can become locked in a tit-for-tat progression up a ladder of aggression. Escalation can easily get out of hand and nobody wins.

An everyday example illustrates the point. My five-year-old daughter announces one morning that she wants to take a packed lunch to school. We do not want to make her one: hot school lunches are good for her. She escalates by saying that she will eat something she knows we don't want her to. We respond calmly, trying to prevent further escalation. She continues that she will not stay for lunch then – another rung up the ladder. We respond that she agreed to have packed lunches until half-term and school lunches for the rest of term. She says that she is breaking the deal. She applies pressure – adopting an irritating whine and making no effort to get dressed although we tell her she is late. In the end she wins – she is the better negotiator.

Our technique, at least, is right – dampen the conflict, don't feed the fire. Absorb the energy of the thrust and let it die away. Don't lose control and make a sudden and unplanned concession. Keep calm. Don't respond with aggression – don't attack the individual. Consider responses such as:

- *Explanation* – Ask them to explain their position. This gives time to think and the opportunity to question their explanation further. It gives the other party time to cool down: it is very hard to maintain a fury for long.
- *Summarize* – Refer back to what has been discussed up to that point and ask them to explain how their new point fits in. This also gives time to think and the opportunity to point to inconsistencies.
- *Control the battlefield* – Switch to discussing other issues, ideally points of agreement – reinforce areas of agreement and benefits. If you can force a broader discussion the attack is dissipated and issues are traded. Even tough negotiators find it hard to maintain the attack when confronted with agreements attained, benefits they have won and issues remaining.

- *Recess* – Seek a recess to consider. This gives time to think and to cool down but it must be proposed with dignity, without giving the impression of panic.
- *Accept blame* – Even if you are not wrong but don't capitulate, don't show weakness. With humans, unlike animals, submission and weakness often leads to renewed attack. A response along the lines of 'I am terribly sorry, I didn't mean to give you that impression ...' or 'I am sorry, that was my mistake but I have some suggestions for correcting it ...' may take the edge off an attack. Don't say, 'I'm sorry you feel like that ...' which implies you are only sorry that they are wrong. If you say you are sorry it must be for some fault of yours and not of theirs. Acknowledge the feelings of others, people appreciate having their emotions recognized: ' I understand why you are angry ...'

Once launched, it is hard to pull out of an attack. The aggressor may need a concession to save face to permit them to be more reasonable: give something that is not too important.

## Your use of aggression

The creative use of aggression can include threats, pressure and the ultimatum.

### Threat

All negotiation contains a threat. 'If we don't reach agreement then ...' However, threats carry the risk of escalation either through deadlock or retaliation. People can respond badly whatever the price; dignity is a rational objective in commerce, alongside profit. Consider also your future relationships. Do you have to live with these people and if they are offended will future service be impaired?

Before issuing a threat always consider:

- *Is the threat credible?* Never issue empty threats that will not be believed.
- *What options are there?* What will you do if they say no?

Threats can be reinforced in many ways, to make them stronger; legal proceedings can be initiated or a new product launched or a rent left unpaid. If used too much threats lose their effectiveness and the victim tests for a bluff – yet the purpose of a threat is not to carry it out.

How do you respond to a threat?

1. Evaluate the threat – What is the cost (to them as well as you) if carried out and what are your options?
2. Your possible responses are – stand firm, give in, bluff or bypass the whole issue by broadening negotiation. 'I understand why you are so concerned about delivery times but consider the overall package of price, quality and delivery ...'

## Pressure

A threat is designed not to be carried out but pressure is the exercise of power, often in a different area from the matter under negotiation. Thus, a trade union may be unhelpful on overtime working when it really seeks an agreement on basic pay rates.

## Ultimatum

An ultimatum is more formal than a threat and its main ingredient is a deadline. It is a 'do this by then or else'.

Ultimatums are effective when you are prepared to act, because success depends upon the other party believing you. An element of theatre is therefore used to convince them that you are serious. A successful ultimatum requires a credible threat, a determination to carry it out, a clear statement of a simple response required and a deadline.

If you cover several issues you invite a response such as 'We will agree to this and that but not to items three and four ...' That puts you back into negotiating detail and it is difficult to use an ultimatum twice. The answer to an ultimatum must be yes or no and not 'yes but'.

## Breaking the logjam

Many negotiations reach a point where they seem to be stuck and everyone is at a loss to think how to break out of the circle. The parties are like two armies locked in battle, with neither able to gain the upper hand and both equally unable to withdraw. In the heat of the conflict their attention is so narrowly directed on the detail of the fighting that they may have forgotten what they are fighting to achieve.

A powerful negotiating technique is to join all parties together to try to find ways to resolve a common problem. Of course, this does require the other side to accept some responsibility for the issue. If they respond with 'That's your problem' then you have to show how if your problem cannot be solved then there is no deal. It cannot be emphasized too often that, in order to resolve problems and break stalemates, the real issue must be clear, not just the surface appearance. Dig deep – ask yet again 'What is this deal really all about, are we stuck on some side issue?'

Another technique for breaking logjams is to call in the heavy artillery. A company chairman behind the scenes may be brought in. They can make concessions that you do not want to do openly, giving the appearance of overruling you. In other circumstances the chairman can make concessions that are beyond your authority. The chairman may attend only for clearing major logjams and may still leave you with problematic detail to resolve.

## Saving face

In a deadlock allow the other party to retain their dignity or they may reject perfectly satisfactory deals rather than lose face. There are two ways of helping the other party to accept they can make a concession:

1. *Give a concession in exchange* – Something trivial may be enough to show the boss.
2. *Sensitive use of words* – Say 'I am pleased this information has helped us reach a compromise' not 'I am pleased you have agreed that one.'

## The heat of battle

What do you do about that unfortunate word or phrase that slips out?

1. *Go back* – If necessary go back into a room you have left and admit your mistake. Forget your embarrassment, the only question is whether going back will do any good.
2. *Reinterpret* – Some things that we say can be undone by saying that we did not mean quite what the other party takes us to have meant.

There may be reasons for fighting hard to win a point that does not really matter. Sometimes you press for a point only to be in a position to trade it later or to make a display of fighting. We may fight only to prevent the other side thinking we are weak. Even in the midst of battle keep calm and retain a sense of proportion. This can be hard to do when emotions are engaged but can be achieved by concentrating upon your interests and not on the argument or on the people.

## The momentum of the deal

Deals have a pace of their own. If the pace slows people become jaded and bored and in their frustration they stick more firmly to their positions. But if we see rapid progress we are encouraged and this boosts our energy and enthusiasm. We work harder to achieve a solution and are more ready to make concessions.

If negotiations drag on they are less likely to succeed: it is better to stop and to revive them at a later stage than to let them continue falteringly. Don't let a meeting finish without progress of some sort that will create a positive mood.

## Concessions

Before making a concession ask 'Is it really necessary?'

- *Has your proposal been rejected?* Often negotiators concede before it is necessary. Silence in response to a proposal or a comment like 'You surely aren't serious!' is often enough to get a better offer. Don't fall for it. Once you make a concession without being asked for it or a second concession before getting a response to the first, there is no reason for them to do anything other than wait to see what will happen next.
- *Do you understand what parts of your proposal are unacceptable and why?* Until you have established that the other party really has rejected your proposal and what parts of it, you cannot know what to concede! Don't reduce your price when it was the delivery date that was the problem. Find out what the other party really expects. Then and only then make moves towards their needs.

### Pace of concessions

It is almost always better to make many relatively small

adjustments to a negotiating position than to make large leaps. In a simple bidding situation for a property you offer 100 and they ask for 1000. Realizing that you bid too low you rebid 300. This is such a large jump, achieved so quickly, that it signals an ability to move a lot further. If your bottom-line price is only 350 then you have created a problem for yourself because they now expect a further substantial move which you cannot make. As you get closer to your bottom line so the increases in successive bids should become smaller, signalling to the other side that you are reaching your final figure.

## Reciprocity and conditionality

Seek a return for any concession. 'Well, that's a difficult one for me to accept because ... but we may be able to accommodate it if ...'

Negotiation is about trading based upon the different values that people place on different things. Therefore don't be too fastidious to enter into trading. *If you don't ask you don't get.*

If you are the one confronted with the demand for reciprocity ask yourself:

1. Would you have expected anyway to win the point?
2. Is what you are being asked to give of equal value to what has been conceded?
3. How vital is the point to you?

It is easy for the other party to concede points of no value to them and to demand in response something of significant value to you. Resist emotional blackmail when there is no logical link between trading point A for point B.

The *conditional* approach is a very powerful variety of this technique. They are phrased the other way around: 'If you are able to agree to ... then we could certainly talk about ...'

The strength of the approach is that you do not have to give the concession first and the offer can be vaguely worded. 'If you can agree to ... then I believe we would be able to move on ...'

## Timing of concessions

If a move is made too soon then a signal is sent that you are too eager and this will harden the other party's position while, if you leave it too late, the other party will conclude there is no deal to be done and will abandon discussions. If there are many possible accommodations then it is appropriate to maintain a pace of small concessions. However, if there is one major issue of contention then it must be left until the end when any other points can be resolved as well. If the major point is dealt with in the middle of negotiation then it is no longer available to sweep up the many minor issues that will arise. It avoids:

1. The salami approach – The other side gets one concession and then turns to another issue and obtains a concession on that and then turns to another issue ... Eventually the deal is done on terms you would not have accepted if everything had been negotiated together.
2. The momentum of the deal – One concession delivered too soon may be seen as a sign of weakness, encouraging further attacks that lead to a momentum of concessions by one party only. Even if you are prepared to agree to a concession, ask yourself 'Is now the right time to offer it?' If you need something in hand to trade later then maybe you should keep the concession for that.

## Becoming committed

It is easy to become committed to a deal as negotiations progress. This leads to poor deals. Ensure that responsibility is shared with your boss. 'Are you sure you want to go ahead on these terms?'

Everyone expects a deal to be completed, staff and the press are told that one is imminent. Don't. You weaken your position immeasurably if the other side thinks you are obliged to do the deal. It simply encourages them to try to enhance their terms at the very last minute.

Sometimes it is hard to prevent being dragged into the deal as discussions progress; staff find out what is going on, soon competitors and suppliers will know, the business may deteriorate or so much information may have been disclosed to a competitor/buyer that there is no going back. Don't let the other side know you are committed.

## Pressure tactics

Applying pressure may resolve a stalemate. It can throw the other party off-balance, putting you in control and allowing you to make a rapid gain. It is aggressive, unsuited to collaborative negotiations. Its success depends upon being able to muster overwhelming force at a pressure point. If the other party parries your thrust then you are the loser.

### Time pressures

You demand that the other side makes an offer within two days. If they scurry off to fulfil this then you have gained an advantage. They have demonstrated weakness. However, if they respond that they cannot or will not comply then you are on the defensive. You can defer the deadline (showing weakness) or walk out: doubling the stakes. A deadline loses its force if it is not adhered to and you lose credibility.

Deadlines are a two-edged sword. If there is real time pressure then the other party may reverse the pressure on you. They may deliberately delay to run the negotiations close to the line, in the hope that you may make concessions. As the deadline approaches you wonder whether they are gambling or whether they really mean it.

## The end game

The oldest technique in negotiation must be the last-minute attempt to get a concession. This relies upon two things: first, that the other side is ready to agree and is therefore amenable to a small concession; second, that other routes that could be pursued, cheaply and easily have been abandoned.

Being at the end there is little fear of repercussions souring future negotiation phases – since there are none to come. The demand may cause such offence that negotiations break down but, at a late stage, the risk is small. Don't employ it when there will be a continuing relationship, since they may get their own back in later trading.

End games happen frequently in property purchases, because they are one-off deals with a large benefit if the ploy works. 'I can do the deal tomorrow but the bank valuer insists that I am paying too much ...' . Many sales of businesses allow a period for investigation, called 'due diligence', and most result in an attempt to renegotiate. Are they bluffing? There is only one way to find out.

# 8

# TECHNIQUES

Most negotiating techniques are incompatible with seeking a mutually advantageous result. Therefore they suit combative negotiations.

## Instant response

Try to respond instantly to any offer, if only to flag that the point has not necessarily been agreed. If someone offers you 20 per cent commission on a deal, ask for 25 per cent or 30 per cent at once: test whether there is more to go for. If you delay then the tentative figure becomes increasingly solid in the other party's mind. Keep the initiative; an immediate challenge makes them doubt their own decision.

## The hypothetical offer

This can sound a bit wishy-washy. It is an offer phrased along the lines 'What would you say if we offered something like . . .?' It can avoid a deadlock. It is a sighting shot, intended to get a response, perhaps from an uncommunicative negotiator. The other party has to say something in response, which opens the way for further questions and discussion. Suppose they answer 'You'll have to do better than that.' You can ask 'In what particular area?' and they may say 'We can't accept such a late completion', which suggests the rest of the offer *was* acceptable. If they accept too readily then the terms can be tightened. 'We could certainly look at putting that together if you could agree to ...'

## The package deal

A package deal offers a number of benefits but with a number of concessions required in return, all in one portmanteau. It is presented as a take-it-or-leave-it offer, denying the other party the right to take some elements while leaving others. Clearly, some of those elements are unattractive but you believe the good bits outweigh the bad.

The package technique has the attraction of shortening negotiations if it is accepted. However, the other side may refuse the package, leaving you having revealed your hand to no effect. Faced with a package deal try to disentangle some of the elements.

## Avoidance, deferral and abeyance

Avoidance of an issue or proposal may be employed by both sides many times in the same meeting. 'Yes, that is an important point but before we deal with that we need to ...' Some suppliers, facing renegotiation of contracts, take this prevarication to an art form, delaying giving straight answers for an interminable time. The reasons are:

1. Hoping the victim may give up in frustration (or change job before any progress is made).
2. A genuine need – Occasionally an issue may genuinely need other things settled first.
3. A tactical desire to get other points to trade first.
4. To gain time to think. If you are on the defensive then you have every reason to defer a difficult issue.

If the technique is used against you, as it surely will be – many times – the best ways of handling it are by:

■ Power

> A supplier was being pressed for a price reduction on their services. Months of detailed debate were getting nowhere. Finally the finance director rang the supplier. 'We want a price reduction. I am not interested in your detailed reasons why we are being wrong and unreasonable. We want to pay less. You come to see me tomorrow with a proposal.'

■ Confrontation – 'Why can't we deal with that now?' Find out why the other party wants to defer discussion. If there is a good reason then flagging it at least prevents it being forgotten. 'OK, let me make a note of that so that we do address it.'
■ Detailed argument – This is the weakest method but, if you are patient, well informed and clever then you may be able to head them off at every side-alley they try.

## The parking lot

If you cannot reach agreement on a point put it to one side (into the parking lot), gathering such issues together and dealing with them at the end. You may end up with a list of six or seven unresolved issues which can be bartered.

There have been occasional times when I have argued long and hard about completely bogus points in order to have something to trade at the end. This can make you appear unreasonable and you may enter a cycle of aggression, encouraging the other side to be difficult on other issues. You may both end up with lists of bogus points held for negotiation.

The parking lot for issues will have to be emptied at some time, so don't set it up for its own sake. If you have too much to resolve at the end then you have gained nothing except a reordering of items for discussion.

## Wear them down

I was involved in a negotiation that continued from Friday morning, throughout the day. We took a break on Saturday and reconvened on Sunday morning and then continued through the night and, with a break for a few hours on Monday morning, went through the day, ending with agreement at eleven o'clock that night. Our lawyer went through masses of documents with painstaking thoroughness, never seeming to tire or to lose interest in the detail. In contrast, the principal on the other side was unwell, obviously worn out and clearly not following all that was going on. Stamina won us important points; don't underestimate it.

If people on the other side are tiring more than you, press on and resist suggestions for a break. Argue that the momentum of the negotiations, which are going so well, will be lost if there is a recess. On the other hand, if you or your team are tiring then demand a break from the negotiations. Even a short break to get some air is valuable.

## Chipping away

Some people will seek a constant stream of small concessions on a wide range of issues, continuing in parallel with the main negotiation on more substantive issues. They will keep the negotiations open for as long as possible in order to achieve this, delaying final signature and possibly even continuing thereafter. This can be extremely irritating. They never quite push you too far in one go.

If you are in a position of strength use threats or an

ultimatum to cut through this technique. An emotional outburst may stop it but a determined adversary may return to it. Confront the other party despite the risk of negotiations breaking down, because unless you stop the chipping away you will lose out. The technique is bound to annoy and can provoke retaliation after the deal is concluded.

## Keep it simple

The old 'KISS' adage ('Keep It Simple, Stupid') is useful for us all. It is too easy to be dragged into a very complex deal through trying to accommodate the other party. The absolute certainty is that complex deals are harder to do than simple ones. They become difficult to follow and trying to trace the interconnections of the various issues becomes a nightmare. The likelihood is that, in trying to accommodate the other party's needs you are simply obscuring the fact of a fundamental difference.

## The dilemma of 'No'

'No' can be the hardest and the easiest word to use. Poor negotiators say no because they lack imagination and don't make the effort to discover the deal waiting to be done. It is often easier to report back to head office that a deal was not possible. Poor negotiators set out their terms and stick to them. Good negotiators find ways to do deals.

Some people are too keen to do a deal and will not say 'no' when only a poor one is available. These personalities are often referred to as accommodators or avoiders. Personal relationships matter more to them than to most people and they will do almost anything to avoid a row. If you recognize that you are not good at saying 'no' use intermediaries to negotiate for you. If you recognize the trait in others, limit their authority.

## Commitment

Commitment is a negotiating technique in its own right. The union negotiator makes an announcement that makes it impossible to conclude an agreement on less favourable terms. 'I'll not come back with less than 5 per cent!' These moves put pressure on the other side but they are a form of doomsday weapon because they risk creating a loss for everyone. The technique is a version of the ancient custom of an invading army literally burning their boats on the beach. The attackers have no option but to proceed and the defenders know that their opponents cannot retreat. If the deal is unacceptable to you as the 'defender' seek a form of presentation that allows the other side to save face.

## The relief strategem

This technique starts with one party adopting a harsh and unbending approach which threatens to deadlock the negotiations. Usually this will be a shock, either because no disagreement was expected or because of the extreme position. The victim feels that there is no way out of the impasse. However, following the meeting the first party will come back and make an offer that is acceptable. This creates such a relief due to the release of tension that the victim immediately accepts.

When this technique is used against you remember you seldom have to give an immediate answer. The other side have made a concession – there may be further concessions to be won. If you try for more and fail to get it then it is unlikely that the deal already on offer will be withdrawn.

# 9

# WINNING THE PEACE

## The aftermath of the meeting

The negotiating meeting is over, how did it go? Was there progress towards your objectives or did you lose? The result of each meeting is the starting point for the next, but the decisions may not be irrevocable. Concessions can be withdrawn, albeit at the risk of impaired relationships, agreements may be interpreted differently, facts on the ground can be changed. In these ways the next meeting may start from a better set of positions than you thought.

It is embarrassing to go back and renegotiate and the other party will try to make you feel bad about it. They will call your honour and integrity into question, hint at legal action, challenge the new information, etc. Therefore remain *focused* on your own interests and not on emotional blackmail. If the deal is no longer right for you *don't be afraid to walk away*!

*Make it easy for the other party*. Give reasons for the changes before saying how you want the terms altered. Sympathize with their frustration and anger. 'I understand why you feel angry, we are also very upset that circumstances have changed in this way ...'

## Making the deal stick

*Your best chance of making a deal work is not to get it*

*wrong in the first place!* Completing negotiations and shaking hands, or even signing a document is not the end, it is often a beginning. Before leaving the room ensure that everyone agrees on what has been agreed. If there are points of substance or of detail that will need to be finalized later, make sure that there is a list of them and that everyone is aware of what needs to be done to make the deal work. There are three broad areas in which a deal may not stick.

## Turning to the detail ...

A deal in principle may be followed up by detailed negotiation which may reveal intractable problems. There is an old saying that 'The devil is in the detail.'

## The fudge factor

Things can be difficult during the negotiation, discussion has been going on for hours, you are tired, you forgot to tell your spouse that you would be so late and that is the fourth time that the other party has repeated that identical argument. The temptation is to fudge: to agree a form of words that does not resolve the problem but allows you to move on.

Many deals lack clarity, deliberately or not. While fudge may be the right course of action in some circumstances, it can be fraught with danger for actually making the deal stick. You can go straight from the negotiating table to the law courts, which is in nobody's interests.

## Living together afterwards

Once people shake hands on a deal and then fight through the paperwork to emerge with signed contracts, they break open the champagne and celebrate the conclusion. In many cases that is not the conclusion at all.

If a deal is fundamentally against the interests of one party then enforcing it may turn into a nightmare. The practical reality is that it is almost impossible to cover every possible contingency and enforcement may swallow an enormous amount of management time. The party wishing to renege will continue pushing to the edge of what they can get away with. Reach agreements that are fair to all parties because human ingenuity at escape is remarkable: or make sure that you can collect your debt!

Making a deal stick, when there is a continuing relationship demands an unambiguous contract and a good measure of goodwill on both sides. Over-negotiation may prove a bad mistake in the long term. Negotiators may deliberately insert terms into a contract that will give them an opportunity to break it in the future. They may be devious in achieving this and only meticulous attention to detail achieves an unambiguous and watertight contract.

---

**Tips for managing the aftermath of negotiation**

- Make notes for yourself of what is agreed; who is to do what and when.
- Tell the staff who helped you prepare what happened – they may still have something to contribute.
- Postpone implementation of decisions reached, if you disagree, to allow the oppor-tunity for revision.
- If you won a point and were given responsibility to do something, do it quickly; create facts that are hard to go back on.
- Check the minutes: have them written your way. If you lost you may want your view recorded. The precise wording of a minute may be important; without committing forgery, the emphasis may be important to you.
- Follow up with meeting partners.

---

> A single person, supported by a review mechanism, should have unambiguous responsibility for making sure things are done and for pestering others to get them to do their parts.

If the negotiation has not resulted in a contract, write notes of what has been agreed and circulate these to all parties as soon as possible afterwards, to ensure that everyone really is in agreement. If you draft these meeting notes you are able to add or detract weight from particular issues. While a 'Heads of Agreement' is a flawed device to achieve this, because interpreting the document can be a whole negotiation on its own, they may be better than nothing. If the agreement is clear and its terms fairly simple Heads can be the best way to ensure progressing the results of the meeting.

## Leave something for your opponent

A dominating negotiator is one who always goes out to win. This tough negotiator will get the best terms possible, squeezing the last drop from the other party, who is left with a barely acceptable deal. But is this the best thing to do? To this success-driven person, the question is hard to comprehend.

The loser who has succumbed to the tough negotiator will search for ways to recover lost ground. There is the additional incentive to have a go at this person who has humiliated them. The service supplier cuts down on the free advice that was being offered before and accountants begin to charge for every telephone call. In the end the loser may end up a winner, having clawed back more than was lost. Even if there remains a benefit to the tough negotiator the atmosphere of guerrilla warfare has its own hidden costs.

## Saving face

Always try to find a way for the other party to save face if you defeat them. In warfare, even the ancient writers advised leaving an escape route for a defeated army. Without one, confronted by certain death, the enemy fights to take as many as possible with them. If you allow something for injured pride and for them to show to their colleagues then agreement is more likely and the deal is more likely to stick.

It costs very little to be humble after a successful negotiation. It is not really necessary to rub the other party's face in the mud: make it look as if you lost something. Emphasize the mutual benefits and the concessions you have made. Don't whoop for joy and point your finger at the vanquished. A senior figure involved in corporate mergers and acquisitions once advised me to 'be humble on the way up, you never know who you might meet on the way down'.

## Mending fences

After a tough negotiation try to rebuild damaged relationships. Demonstrating respect for the 'opponent' relieves some of their pain. Even shaking hands after a bruising meeting can have that effect if there is sincerity. The important thing is not just to go through a social ritual but to seek reconciliation. If you have to deal with someone again then, whether you lost, won or drew, it usually helps the process if you are on reasonably amicable terms.

# The 30 Minutes Series

The *Kogan Page 30 Minutes Series* has been devised to give your confidence a boost when faced with tackling a new skill or challenge for the first time.

So the next time you're thrown in at the deep end and want to bring your skills up to scratch or pep up your career prospects, turn to the *30 Minutes Series* for help!

*Titles available are:*

30 Minutes Before Your Job Interview
30 Minutes Before a Meeting
30 Minutes Before a Presentation
30 Minutes to Boost Your Communication Skills
30 Minutes to Brainstorm Great Ideas
30 Minutes to Deal With Difficult People
30 Minutes to Succeed in Business Writing
30 Minutes to Master the Internet
30 Minutes to Make the Right Decision
30 Minutes to Make the Right Impression
30 Minutes to Plan a Project
30 Minutes to Prepare a Job Application
30 Minutes to Write a Business Plan
30 Minutes to Write a Marketing Plan
30 Minutes to Write a Report
30 Minutes to Write Sales Letters

*Available from all good booksellers*
For further information on the series, please contact:

Kogan Page, 120 Pentonville Road, London N1 9JN
Tel: 0171 278 0433 Fax: 0171 837 6348